His Name Was Raoul Wallenberg

www.hmhbooks.com
Book design by YAY! Design.
The text of this book is set in Granjon.
The maps are by Rachel Newborn.
Photo credits are on page 135.

Library of Congress Cataloging-in-Publication Data
Borden, Louise.
  His name was Raoul Wallenberg / by Louise Borden.
    p. cm.
  ISBN 978-0-618-50755-9
  1. Wallenberg, Raoul, 1912–1947—Juvenile literature. 2. Righteous Gentiles in the
Holocaust—Biography—Juvenile literature. 3. Holocaust, Jewish (1939–1945)—Juvenile
literature. 4. World War, 1939–1945—Jews—Rescue—Juvenile literature. 5. Righteous
Gentiles—Sweden—Biography—Juvenile literature. I. Title.
  D804.66.W35B67 2012
  940.53'18092—dc22
  [B]
                          2011003451

Manufactured in China
LEO 10 9 8 7 6 5 4 3 2 1
4500322356

NOTE

In the years before and during World War II, many nations referred
to their representative to a foreign country as a "minister" and to the
building and staff as a "legation." These are the terms I have used in this
book. Since World War II, the terms "ambassador" and "embassy" have
been most commonly used.

The city of Istanbul, Turkey, was called Constantinople until 1930.

The term *schutzpass* is German. The plural of this word in German would
be *schutzpasse* (not *schutzpasses*, which is Anglicized). In this book I have
used the German plural.

HIS NAME WAS RAOUL WALLENBERG

COURAGE, RESCUE, AND MYSTERY DURING WORLD WAR II

BY LOUISE BORDEN

Houghton Mifflin Books for Children
Houghton Mifflin Harcourt
Boston New York 2012

FOR NINA AND GUY
AND FOR THE YOUNG PEOPLE OF THE WORLD

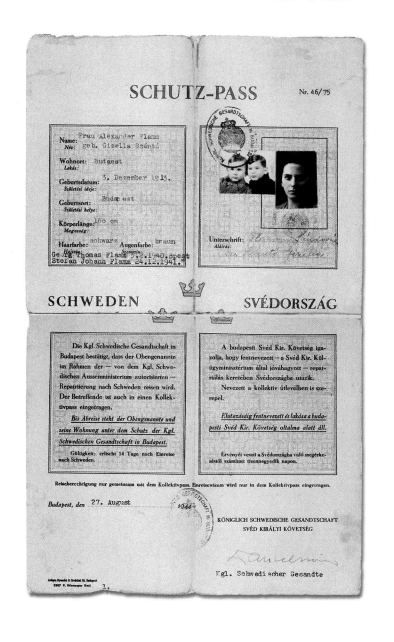

CONTENTS

1 Inge Böös 2 Anders Hagström er 3 K. A. Sundhvist 4 Arne Wallin

5 Bengt Rosenberg 6 Sten Möller 7 Torsten Lundin 8 Axel Trotzig

9 Axel von Heijne 10 Bengt Tornblad 11 Georg Lindner 12 Torsten Holmgren

13 Gunnar Wretblad 14 Rolf von Krusenstierna 15 Johan Banér 16 Rolf Öy.

17 Åke Gustafsson 18 Stig Andrén 19 Raoul. Wallenberg. 20 Sven Lagerqvist

21 Paul Isberg 22 Olof Agrén 23 Göran Tönnberg 24 Claes Lundqvist

25 Olof Carlson 26 Curt Krook 27 Curt Frölén 28 Börje Lindberg

29 Rolf af Klintberg 30 Hans Sjöqvist 31 Bo Stenberg

Raoul Wallenberg's class photo from Stockholm, circa 1921.

Look closely
at this faded school picture from Sweden.

Find the student whose number is 19
and match 19 to his signature.
Read it aloud. Let it echo.

19 *Raoul. Wallenberg.*

It's a name for the world to remember.

Now you,
and others,
can become the storytellers
of this boy's remarkable life . . .

SWEDEN

1912–1922

Early one Sunday
in August of 1912,
a baby was born near Stockholm, Sweden,
on the island of Lidingö.

His grandmother Wising's summer house,
called Kappsta,
is no longer there.

Kappsta, the birthplace of
Raoul Wallenberg.

All that is left today
is an old foundation
open to the sky . . .

Foundation of Kappsta. The
summer house was destroyed
by fire in the 1930s.

Raoul as a baby.

Raoul's father, Raoul Oscar
Wallenberg, circa 1911.

and a path that winds to the Baltic Sea.
Nearby
in a stand of beech trees
lie the silent stones of Viking graves.

This Swedish boy,
born on an island,
would grow up
to become a hero to many.

His name was Raoul Wallenberg . . .

In 1912,
Wallenberg
was a famous family name in Sweden.
The Wallenbergs were bankers . . .
builders of industry . . .
diplomats . . .
and artists.
They took pride in the Swedish flag
and used their talents
and their wealth
in quiet ways.

The baby's mother, Maj,
named him Raoul Gustaf Wallenberg
after her husband,
a handsome officer in Sweden's navy.
But little Raoul would never know his father,
who died of cancer
three months before his son was born.

3

Maj Wallenberg,
a widow at age twenty,
hid her sadness and hung five small pictures
painted by her husband
on the walls of the baby's nursery at Kappsta.
She wanted her son to see the beauty in the world,
and the joy.

Raoul and his mother, Maj.

Raoul's homeland, in the north of Europe,
reached beyond the Arctic Circle.
Stockholm, its capital,
was nearly seven hundred years old,
built on fourteen islands.
Nearby in the Baltic was an archipelago,
one of the largest in the world:
24,000 more islands . . . and skerries with heather,
swept by the wind.

MAP OF SCANDINAVIA
c. 1905

Arctic Circle

Atlantic Ocean

NORWAY

Kristiania *

SWEDEN

Stockholm

North Sea

Øresund Strait

DENMARK

Copenhagen

GERMANY

POLAND

Gulf of Bothnia

FINLAND

Helsinki

Baltic Sea

RUSSIA

*NAME OF OSLO FROM 1877–1925

During the long Swedish winters,
thick ice locked in the boats against Stockholm's quays,
and in midwinter
there were only about six hours of light each day.
In spring and summer,
the city's gold spires gleamed in the sunshine
and its gardens were full of flowers.

An aerial view of Stockholm, Sweden.

After the loss of her husband
and the birth of her son,
in late 1912,
Maj had another change in her life:
her beloved father, Per Wising,
passed away.
Now Maj's mother was also a widow.

Maj Wallenberg looked to the future.
She moved from Kappsta
to central Stockholm
and there she read stories to young Raoul
in her flat at 7–9 Linnégatan,
or took him by the hand
to explore the trees and paths in the Humlegården,
half a block from their apartment.

Childhood photos of Raoul.

Always,
he was her treasure.

Raoul's other grandfather,
Gustaf Oscar Wallenberg,
was to become an important guide
in the boy's life.
This grandfather was a man of bold ideas.
He'd already built a train tunnel,
a spa hotel near Saltsjöbaden,
and his own villa by the sea.
Now Gustaf lived in Tokyo
and was Sweden's minister to Japan.
He wrote letters of counsel to Maj in Stockholm,
and when Raoul was almost four,
Gustaf and his wife, Annie,
returned home to meet their grandson.
Raoul called Gustaf *"Farfar,"*
the Swedish name for grandfather.

Raoul with his grandfather, circa 1916.

Raoul with his mother, Maj, in Stockholm.

Farfar was old, with his pocket watch
and silvery beard,
and Raoul was young.
But they were both Wallenbergs.
This was their strong bond.

In 1918,
when her son was six,
Maj remarried . . . to Fredrik von Dardel.
Now Raoul had a father in his life,
and Mr. von Dardel was like a *true* father.
Three weeks after Raoul's seventh birthday,
his brother,
Guy von Dardel,
was born.

Raoul and his younger brother, Guy.

And two years later, in 1921,

little Nina,

on an early March day.

On the fourth floor of 43 Riddargatan,

the "Street of the Knight,"

the von Dardel home echoed with the roar of a lion

or the chirping of birds,

for Raoul was an actor who could mimic animals

as well as the voices of people.

Nina and Guy were his loyal audience,

and as the oldest child in the family,

Raoul gave them both his patience and his love.

The apartment home of the von
Dardel family in Stockholm.

From his bedroom window high above the street,
Raoul could point to the stars on clear Swedish nights
and by day,
to the small statue that gave Riddargatan its name.

A statue on the street in Stockholm
where Raoul grew up.

He loved books, and discovering new facts,
and by his tenth birthday
Raoul had read every volume of the *Nordiska Encyclopedia*.

Raoul was also an artist . . .
like the father he'd been named for.
When he painted a picture of a horse
with unusual hues,
and gave it to Guy,
his family discovered that Raoul was colorblind.

But he never stopped drawing,
and his school papers were filled with scribbles and sketches.

With a good ear for music
and a fine voice as well,
Raoul joined the select boys' choir
of a famous Stockholm church.
He already knew stories from the Bible;
in the choir he sang soaring hymns.

Sweden's capital was growing with the new century
and its streets were busy with building and trade.
After school
Raoul often stopped to study an ancient doorway,
or tracked mud home from construction sites,
where he had asked carpenters and bricklayers
a dozen questions about their craft.

A street on Gamla Stan.

Indeed,
young Raoul Wallenberg stood apart from his classmates
in his constant curiosity.
He wanted to know how the world worked,
and he felt life in a deep way.

During his childhood years,
Raoul and his school friend Rolf af Klintberg
flew kites in the Baltic breezes
or bicycled through the King's Park,
the Kungsträdgården,
on their way to the harbor,
where Raoul could name every kind of foreign ship.
Sweden's king and queen lived at the Royal Palace
on Gamla Stan,
an island with a warren of medieval streets.
A few bridges away,
across the shimmering water,
was the new Stadshuset, the city hall.

Buildings on the waterfront in Gamla Stan, Stockholm, Sweden.

From its handsome brick tower,
Raoul could look down on a paint box of houses and boats.
Above him,
three gold crowns, the symbol for Sweden,
shone in the sun.

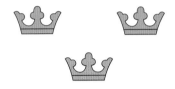

Stockholm.

This was the watery city where Raoul Wallenberg grew up . . .
and where white sails dotted the horizon
on blue sky days.

TRAVELS

1923–1930

R aoul's grandfather was now Sweden's minister to Turkey.
Gustaf Wallenberg wanted Raoul to find his independence,
so in 1923,

the year he turned eleven,

Raoul left Sweden alone and unafraid,

with the royal seal of three crowns stamped on his passport.

Already, he was becoming an observer of the world.

Raoul's 1923 Swedish passport photo.

From Vienna to Constantinople,

he rode on the famous Orient Express,

and as the towns and farms of central Europe flashed past,

Raoul never knew that his grandfather

had paid the train conductors

to discreetly watch over him.

After this exotic trip to the capital of Turkey,
Raoul returned home to 43 Riddargatan
and his school life in Sweden.
There were summer picnics at Kappsta,
and as the siblings grew older,
Raoul cheered on Guy, who could ice skate with a sail,
and helped Nina learn to ski.

He loved the sea
and sailed with his cousins
from island to island in the archipelago.
This Wallenberg had stamina and energy—
and he could skate across a frozen lake
even when his friends had grown tired
and turned back.

Raoul Wallenberg at age twelve.

One summer,
his grandfather sent him to England
to live with a clergyman, Mr. Vigers.
There Raoul studied English,
and found that the books in his host's library
were filled with stories of exciting adventures.
The next July,
when Raoul was seventeen,
he lived with a family in Thonon-Les-Bains,
a town on Lake Geneva in France.
Each morning,
Madame Bourdillon taught grammar lessons
to Raoul and her other boarders.
One of them, László Petö,
became Raoul's friend.
The students practiced French vocabulary,
and after class, hiked up steep trails in the Alps.
Raoul carried a sketchbook in his rucksack
and wrote letters to his grandfather
about the mountain views.

Raoul had an ear for languages.
As a student in Stockholm,
he studied German
and earned excellent marks in Russian.
He took pride in his Wallenberg name
and set goals for himself in his education.
The world was a big place
and Raoul wanted to be ready for that world.

AMERICA

1931–1935

In 1930,
Raoul graduated from high school
and took his required nine months
of Swedish military training.
He returned to France
to take courses in Poitiers,
and then in September 1931,
Raoul boarded the *Kungsholm*
in Gothenberg, Sweden,
and sailed to New York City.

Raoul Wallenberg,
high school graduate.

The *Kungsholm*.

It was time to attend college.
He wanted to study architecture in the United States,
the land of energy and ideas,
and had chosen the University of Michigan,
with many kinds of students,
not just the rich.
Gustaf Wallenberg, still living in Turkey,
hoped that his grandson could find "the spirit of America"
as he himself had, years before.

At Michigan,
Raoul was called "Rudy" by his classmates.
Rudy Wallenberg wore sneakers,
like an American,
and went to the movies twice a week.

After class,
he bicycled along the streets of Ann Arbor
or painted bright pictures
to pin on the walls
of his boardinghouse room.

Raoul as a college freshman.

Soon he joined the debate club
to polish his English.
He became a good speaker . . . and a good listener.

Raoul had a wide circle of friends
but no time for snobs.
He never told anyone that his Wallenberg uncles
Jacob and Marcus
managed the Stockholms Enskilda Bank,
the bank that Raoul's great-grandfather
had founded,
and were often guests of the king
at the Royal Palace.

Right away,
his architecture professors
saw Raoul's gift for drawing.
He copied the details of cathedrals in pencil,
learned how to design space,
and studied exciting new skyscrapers.

21

The reading room at the
University of Michigan
Law Library, where many
students study.

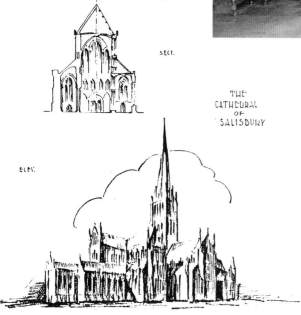

SECT.

THE
CATHEDRAL
OF
SALISBURY

ELEV.

A drawing by Raoul Wallenberg
for a college assignment.

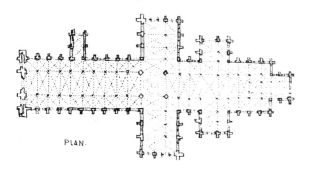

PLAN.

An archway at the University of Michigan.

Raoul on his summer travels. He often wore his college ROTC uniform because he felt it made him look more respectable.

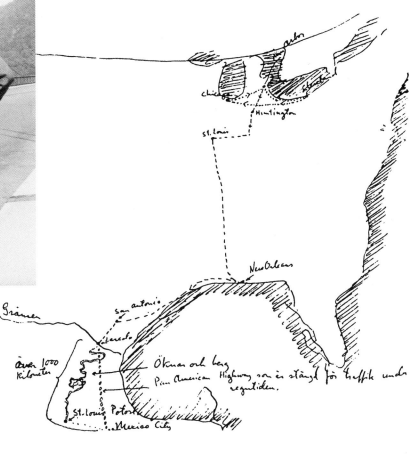

A drawing by Raoul from a travel letter to his mother.

In a letter home to Stockholm,
Raoul wrote to his uncle Marcus Wallenberg:
"Amerika imponerar mycket på mig,"
which means "I am very impressed by America."

These were the years of the Great Depression,
and during school breaks
Raoul hitchhiked around the United States.

He joined the New Yorkers
hurrying through Grand Central Station,
rode the cable cars up San Francisco's steep hills,
and learned the names of many of the nation's small towns.

23

One summer,
Raoul worked at the Swedish exhibit
at Chicago's World Exposition.
While he was hitchhiking back to college,
on a lonely road in Indiana,
some rough men offered him a ride
and then pointed a gun at him
and took his wallet.
Raoul was able to talk his way out of danger.

Another July,
Raoul drove with a friend to Mexico City
in an old Ford truck . . .
and mailed a hand-drawn map of their journey
to his mother, Maj.
Always a keen observer of people and places,
along the way he sold sketches of his travels
to earn pocket money.

Raoul on the steps of Angell Hall
at the University of Michigan.

The next winter,
in January of 1935,
when his architecture studies were almost at an end,
Raoul worked for days drawing a large mural,
full of color,
that his professor hung in the hallway near his office.
Then during the first week of February,
a term early,
Raoul Wallenberg graduated from college with honors.

It was time to leave wonderful America
and go home.

CITIZEN OF THE WORLD

1935–1940

G ustaf Wallenberg wanted Raoul
to become a citizen of the world,
so that summer,
after a reunion with his family,
the young architect took a train from Stockholm to Norway
and boarded the ship *Hammaren*.
Raoul's destination was the tip of South Africa,
in the Southern Hemisphere,
where he arrived on July 8,
a warm winter day.

Raoul spent the next six months
living in Cape Town,
with a view of the ocean and Table Mountain.
There he worked with a Swedish import firm,
bartering products
and traveling to other towns in South Africa.
Gustaf Wallenberg
had more plans for Raoul,
and he wrote to his grandson
advising him to go to Palestine,
in the Middle East.

In February of 1936,
Raoul left Cape Town
with letters of recommendation from South Africa
tucked in his suitcase,
and sailed north on an Italian ship,
the *Duilio,*
headed to the Strait of Gibraltar.

The passenger ship *Duilio*.

Days later,
his boat docked at Genoa.
Now across Europe,
there were rumors of war,
and it was hard to obtain travel papers in Italy to go to Palestine.
At the consulate,
Raoul stated his case clearly and with persistence.
Finally his visa was stamped.

Raoul's grandparents were staying at the Hotel D'Angleterre
in Nice, France,
so Raoul made a quick visit to see Gustaf and Annie Wallenberg
before returning to Genoa
where on February 29,
he boarded a small ship bound for Haifa.
En route,
it put in at Piraeus, Greece,
and Raoul was able to see the ancient buildings in Athens.
Later the ship docked in Alexandria, Egypt,
and that evening Raoul marveled at dozens of lights.

The British warships at anchor
were a powerful sight,
and an omen of the world conflict to come.
In Haifa,
a new city in Palestine by the sea,
Raoul found a job at the Holland Bank
and spoke German and French with his foreign clients.
Daily on the docks of Haifa,
more Jews were arriving in Palestine.
They had left their homes in Nazi Germany
because Adolf Hitler's National Socialist laws
had taken away their rights
and their jobs.

At 18 Arlosorof Street,
the boardinghouse where Raoul lived,
they told stories of beatings and murder.

An ovation for Hitler at the Reichstag, Germany. National Socialism was on the rise.

That fall,
Raoul needed to report
for another month of Swedish military duty,
so he booked passage on a Polish ship, the *Polonia,* to Turkey
and took a train home through Warsaw and Berlin.
Because he had read Hitler's book, *Mein Kampf,*
Raoul sensed the evil plans of the German führer.
When his train passed through stations displaying Nazi banners,
Raoul Wallenberg's face was grim.
In his heart,
he carried the voices of his refugee friends.

Back in Stockholm,
Raoul settled into an apartment on Östermalmsgatan,
near the church where he'd sung as a choirboy,
and the Humlegården.
He began to look for a job.

Then in March of 1937,
Raoul's grandfather Gustaf Wallenberg,
who had returned to Sweden
in fragile health,
died.
Raoul's beloved mentor was gone.
For the next few years,
Raoul Wallenberg drifted without direction . . .
like a sailboat in irons on a glassy sea.

The economy was poor,
and there were no jobs in Stockholm
for an American-trained architect
and no place at the Wallenbergs' bank.

Raoul tried to start two businesses
but lost money.
He couldn't seem to find a steady breeze.

Meanwhile,
the shadow of Nazi goals slowly spread across Europe . . .
and on September 1, 1939,
Germany invaded Poland.

Months later,
in April of 1940,
Hitler's paratroopers made a surprise attack on Sweden's neighbors,
Denmark and Norway.
In May,
his Panzer tanks swept through Holland,
Belgium,
and France.

Hitler and officers in
Paris, France.

Raoul Wallenberg's homeland had been at peace
for a hundred years.
The Swedish government decided to honor that tradition
and stay out of the battles.
During World War II,
only a few nations didn't take sides
and were safe from war.
These were called *neutral countries*.

The rest of Europe fell into dark times.

A German Panzer tank in the snow.

WAR IN EUROPE

1940—1944

Now the Nazi terror of ordinary people began,
and for Jews in the occupied countries,
it grew much worse.

Jews could not hold jobs
or travel . . .
and they were no longer citizens.
They could not worship in their synagogues.
Their money was taken from them.
They had to sew a yellow Star of David on their clothing
so everyone would know their identity.
Jewish children couldn't go to school with non-Jews,
or play with non-Jewish friends.

Jews had to hand over their radios
and bicycles
and cars.
They couldn't walk on the sidewalk.
They couldn't ride on buses or trams.
Families whose great-great-great-grandparents
had been born in these countries
were made to live in ghettos,
where streets were fenced off with locked gates.

The Star of David.

Hitler's plan was to deport all Jews
and send them on trains to concentration camps.
He would work them to death through slave labor,
or kill them in gas chambers.

Thousands
and then millions of people
suffered under the Nazi laws,
and were beaten and killed,
even people who were not Jewish.
Anyone who resisted . . . was arrested or shot.

During these early years of the war,
Raoul Wallenberg was safe in Stockholm.
Every Sunday,
Raoul, Nina, and Guy met their friends at Central Station.
From there they would go to ski or skate or sail . . .
but the war was always a topic.

Skiing in Sweden. Nina is second from left and Raoul is second from right.

One night Raoul took his sister to the British legation
to see a new film in English,
Pimpernel Smith.
Because Sweden was neutral,
the movie couldn't be shown in Swedish theaters.

Raoul and Nina
in 1943.

The story was about a man who helped refugees
escape from the Nazis.
After the film,
Raoul told Nina that someday,
he, too, wanted to do something
to help people in trouble.

In this same year, 1941,
Raoul was living at 12 Bragevägen
and had found a job
working for an export-import business.
The owner was Kálmán Lauer,
a Hungarian Jew who lived in Stockholm.
Mr. Lauer saw in Raoul Wallenberg
the skills of a salesman who could talk and listen . . .
in five languages.
Raoul became Lauer's trade representative,

Raoul's apartment in Stockholm.

and with his neutral passport

traveled around Europe.
He saw the harsh life under German occupation,
and noticed in his quiet way
that the Nazi border guards
were impressed by rules,
and lists.

Twice Raoul took a train to Budapest,
the capital of Hungary,
to buy and sell food products,
and carried letters to Kálmán Lauer's relatives.

In September of 1943,
a few miles across the water from Sweden,
the Jews of occupied Denmark were in great peril.
The Nazis wanted to round up every one of them
and ship them to camps.
On October 1,
the Swedish government,
and the king,
gave permission for thousands of Danes
to cross the Øresund Strait in small boats

Danish Jewish refugees
after their crossing from
Denmark to Sweden.

Fishing boat taking
Jewish refugees from
Falster (Denmark) to Ystad
in Sweden,
September/October 1943.

manned by brave fishermen
and take refuge in Sweden.

When Raoul Wallenberg bicycled
through his peaceful city
or rode the streetcar to work,
the courage and hardships of others
were often on his mind.
More than once,
he gave Swedish kronor for food and warm coats
to refugee families living in Stockholm.

Strandvägen,
where Raoul's office was located,
was one of Stockholm's finest streets.
When Raoul,
now a partner in the Central European Trading Company,
returned from his trading trips
and walked through the elegant gates to 7A,
the notes in his satchel

Kálmán Lauer.

Strandvägen in Stockholm.

were covered with sketches,
and the notes from Budapest
were written in red and green ink.
"With the white paper,
I have the three colors
of your Hungarian flag!"
he told Kálmán Lauer.

Unlike Sweden, Hungary was not a neutral country.
After World War I,
more than half of its land had been given away
to its neighbors in a treaty.
When World War II began,
Hitler promised the leaders of Hungary
that their nation would get that land back.
But . . . there was a price:
Hungary would have to fight on Germany's side
against the Allies and Russia.

From 1941 on,
Hungary sent soldiers to fight for Hitler.

For the first years of the war,
the battles were far away in Russia.
In Budapest,
shopkeepers were busy,
children went to school,
and most Jews went to work like everyone else.
Some lost their jobs
or were sent as laborers to the front
but for the most part,

Budapest's Jews were left alone
because of the actions of old Admiral Miklós Horthy.
Since the Hungarian monarchy had died out
and there was no longer a royal king or queen,
Admiral Horthy had been chosen to serve
as the regent of Hungary.

He had told Hitler that these Jews were *Hungarians,*
that they were his citizens.
In countries like Poland,
France,
and Holland,
Hitler's SS made sure that Jews were deported to camps
and killed.

During these dark times in Europe,
on December 17, 1943, in Stockholm,
Nina von Dardel became a bride.
Her groom, Gunnar Lagergren, was thirty-one,
the same age as Raoul,
who built a lovely arch for the ceremony
and made a speech to the wedding guests
filled with words of a brother's love.

On New Year's Day,
Raoul's family said somber goodbyes
to their sweet Nina.
Gunnar was being sent to Berlin
for a job at the Swedish legation . . .
and Hitler's Germany was a dangerous place
in January of 1944.

THE JEWS OF HUNGARY

MARCH–JUNE 1944

Slowly,
the world began to find out about the death camps in Europe,
and across the Atlantic Ocean,
President Franklin D. Roosevelt
felt that America needed to do *something*.
In January of 1944,
he set up the War Refugee Board.
Its goal was to aid any gypsies or Jews in Europe
who were still alive and being persecuted.
Meanwhile,
American and British planes were bombing Germany.
The Russian army was heading toward Hungary from the east.
Admiral Horthy *knew* that his country was losing,
and he wanted to make peace with the Allies.
But . . .
Hitler didn't trust anyone,
even those on his own side.
His spies in Budapest
told him about Horthy's plans.
In March,
Hitler asked the regent to meet with him
at a castle in Austria.

It was all a trick.

On a Sunday morning,
March 19, 1944,
while Admiral Horthy was on the train
headed back home from the castle,
Hitler's tanks rolled into Budapest
to occupy their *ally,*
Hungary.

Miklós Horthy.

WWII MAP OF WESTERN
EUROPE SEPTEMBER, 1944

Territory occupied by German forces
Territory of Neutrals and Allies

For the first time
there were German soldiers on the streets of the capital.
Horthy was still regent, but he had no power.
Hitler's chosen Hungarian officials dictated the laws,
helped by a group of local pro-Nazis
called the Arrow Cross.
Within weeks,
Jewish people lost their jobs.

They stood in long lines
to hand over their radios and bicycles.
They were not allowed to use the telephone
or ride on city trams.
They couldn't drive cars.
Now they, too,
were forced to sew a yellow star on their clothing.

That spring,
Hitler sent Adolf Eichmann to make plans
for the Hungarian Jews.
In May,
Eichmann began his terrible work,
and decided first to kill all the Jews
who lived in the countryside, in Hungary's villages.
Then he would turn on the Jews living in Budapest.
With the help of local and willing gendarmes,
the German SS rounded up Jewish families
and marched them to train stations,
where Jews were clubbed and pushed into freight cars
meant to carry cattle.

Each car had only one bucket of water
and little food.
With eighty people crammed into each one,
many had to stand.
Some fainted in the summer heat . . .
      some went crazy . . .
            hundreds died.

Every week the trains left Hungary,
44   headed to concentration camps.

More than 450,000 Jews from Hungary's small towns
went to Auschwitz,
a camp in Poland.
There they were killed in gas chambers.
Hitler's evil wish was coming true.
The only Hungarian Jews left
were those who were next on Eichmann's list
to deport and kill:
the 160,000 Jews in Budapest.

Hundreds of desperate people
stood outside the Swedish legation
and other neutral legations in Budapest
and begged for help.
Sweden's minister to Hungary,
Carl Ivan Danielsson,

Carl Ivan Danielsson on the rooftop of the
Swedish legation in Budapest in 1944.

Per Anger on the
roof of the
Swedish legation in
Budapest.

and his colleague Per Anger,
the Swedish legation's second highest official,
began to sign special letters
for any Hungarian Jews
who had Swedish relatives or business connections.

These papers put them under the protection of Sweden.

The small legation staff of five
worked from morning until late at night,
typing up almost seven hundred documents.
But there were *thousands* of Jews without ties to Sweden.

Minister Danielsson sent urgent cables
to the Foreign Ministry in Stockholm.
He needed more staff,
and he needed advice on how to cope
with the growing tragedy.
Around the clock,
those at the Swiss, Portuguese, and Spanish legations
also typed similar letters,
using their official stationery.
All of these diplomats felt moral outrage
at the Nazi methods
and the deportations of thousands of ordinary people.

The letterhead of the Portuguese
legation in Budapest.

LEGAÇÃO DE PORTUGAL NA HUNGRIA
A MAGYARORSZÁGI PORTUGÁL KÖVETSÉG
DIE PORTUGIESISCHE GESANDSCHAFT

The future of Budapest's Jews looked bleak.

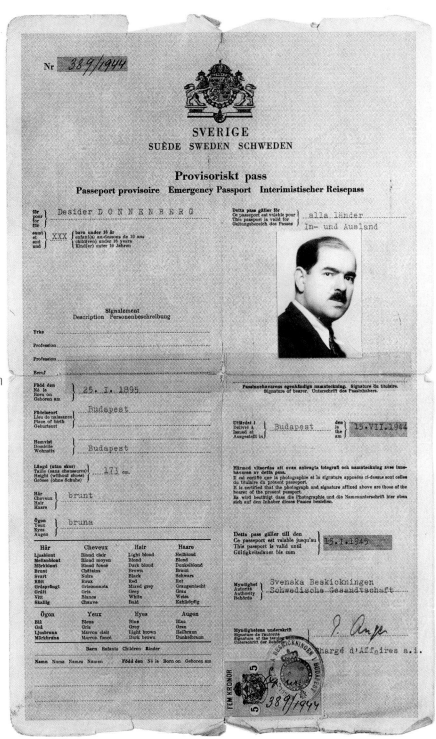

An example of a provisional document issued by the Swedish legation in Budapest.

MISSION TO
BUDAPEST

MAY–JULY 1944

By late May,
in his Stockholm office,
Kálmán Lauer was frantic.
His wife's parents in Hungary had already been put on a train
and deported.
Raoul and his banker uncle, Jacob Wallenberg,
sponsored Lauer
so he could quickly become a Swedish citizen,
hoping this might save the rest of his family.

In June,
many Jews in Budapest
were ordered to mark their apartment buildings with yellow stars.
Soon Eichmann would deport them to Auschwitz, too.

That same month,
the War Refugee Board
sent an American, Iver Olsen,
to Stockholm to find a Swede for a mission to Hungary.
Only a citizen of a neutral country
would have any chance of success
in organizing some kind of help for the Jews.
Count Folke Bernadotte,
a man of compassion
and a cousin of the Swedish king,
was first suggested
as the best person to travel to Budapest.

Count Folke Bernadotte.

But German officials refused to allow him diplomatic status
because of his ties to the royal family.

The American legation
located on Strandvägen
was on the third floor of 7A.
The Central European Trading Company office
was on the fifth floor
and there Mr. Olsen met with Kálmán Lauer,
a man known for his circle of contacts in Hungary.

Could he recommend any Swede
who spoke German or Hungarian?
Who had courage?
Who had been to Budapest?
Instantly,
Lauer gave the American an answer:
"Raoul Wallenberg."

He told Iver Olsen that Raoul was a man
with energy and intelligence,
who knew the world,
who could lead others,
who respected humanity,
who could speak many languages,
who knew Budapest and its people . . .
who had a great heart.

On that June day in 1944
in the office on Strandvägen
the American felt a glimmer of hope.
This Wallenberg fellow seemed to be just the right man
to try something that had never been done before.

A few evenings later,
Olsen, Kálmán Lauer, and Raoul
had dinner at the elegant hotel in Saltsjöbaden
that Raoul's grandfather,
Gustaf Wallenberg,
had built years before.
They talked from seven o'clock at night until five the next morning.

After this detailed session,
Olsen asked Raoul Wallenberg
to meet with the American minister to Sweden,
Herschel Johnson,
who then gave his approval.
Both the War Refugee Board
and the World Jewish Council
would provide funds for the rescue mission.

Raoul in his Swedish
Home Guard uniform.

A few days later,
Raoul was on weekend duty
in the Swedish Home Guard near Stockholm
when a messenger arrived with a note
from the Foreign Ministry:
"Sergeant No. 1775 45/3C
R. G. Wallenberg is to report immediately . . ."

Quickly he left the army grounds on his bicycle
and pedaled back to his apartment . . .
ready to begin his vital assignment.
Raoul was given official reports to study,
and he knew as he turned the pages
that every day counted in saving Budapest's Jews.

Raoul devised his own special code

to use for letters to send back to Kálmán Lauer,
and had a photo taken for his diplomat's passport.
With this document,
he would be treated with respect
and have the protection of the Swedish king
and his government.

Raoul's Swedish diplomatic
passport.

Raoul Wallenberg knew he would need to work in his own way . . .
He would even use money
to bribe the police or officials in Hungary
if that could save Jewish lives.

He didn't want to have to answer to *anyone* in Budapest . . .
even Minister Danielsson.
The Swedish government and King Gustav V
read Raoul's list of rules
and agreed.

King Gustav of Sweden

Then . . . while Raoul was packing for his mission,
something important happened in Geneva, Switzerland.

A diplomat named George Mandell-Mantello
was given a copy of secret papers
written by several Jews who had escaped from Auschwitz.
Their letter had details of the terrible murders there.
Mr. Mandell-Mantello made dozens of copies of the report
and sent them to newspapers and diplomats in Geneva.

Soon the news spread.

President Roosevelt sent an angry warning
to Admiral Horthy
via the neutral Swiss.
You must stop these evil trains, or else.
When Hungary loses the war,
she will be punished . . .
just like Hitler's Germany.
The pope in Rome also sent a cable.

A page from Raoul's passport, with his name spelled as "Raul."

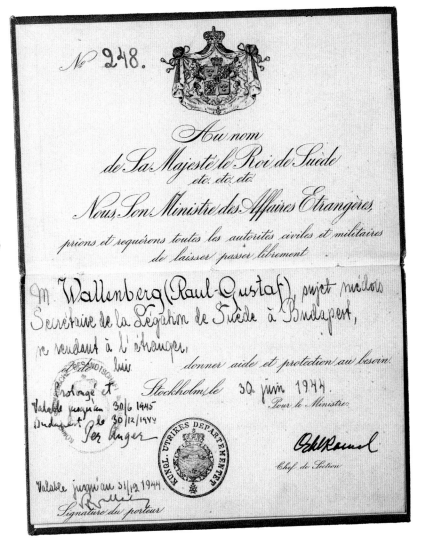

On June 30,
the day that Raoul's new passport
was signed and stamped,
the Swedish government asked the king
to send his own strong words
to Admiral Horthy.
Minister Danielsson and Per Anger
buttoned their formal morning coats
and put on their top hats
to hand the king's message,
written in French,
the official language of diplomats,
to Horthy . . .

and the world waited to see what would happen.

The regent of Hungary pondered the protests,
especially the one sent by King Gustav.
Then,
because he had much respect for neutral Sweden,
the old leader *finally* stood up to Hitler
and ordered a halt to the evil trains.

That same week,
Raoul Wallenberg was to depart for Budapest.

Maj and Fredrik von Dardel, and Kálmán Lauer,
drove Raoul to the Bromma Airport in Stockholm,
where he boarded a courier plane.
He wore a warm jacket and hiking boots,
and carried two rucksacks,
a sleeping bag,

and a revolver that he'd bought secondhand.
"Secondhand to save the government money . . .
and the revolver will give me courage,"
Raoul told his business friend, with his usual wit.

From the plane's window,
Raoul saw the silver gleam of the Baltic Sea
and the archipelago he'd sailed
with his Wallenberg cousins
and Nina and Guy.
Sweden . . . his beautiful and safe homeland.

An aerial view
of Sweden.

Now he was being sent by America
and his own country
to help strangers in wartime,
miles away.
Since childhood,
a sense of knowing right from wrong
had been a steady compass for Raoul Wallenberg.
This,
more than the gun in his pocket,
would be his courage.

The plane turned south from Sweden
and headed to Berlin.
There,
Raoul's brother-in-law, Gunnar Lagergren,
was still working at the Swedish legation.
Nina, and other neutral Swedes,
were bringing kettles of soup
to those in need.
Every morning and evening,
British and American bombers flew over Berlin
and pounded Hitler's proud capital to rubble.

The Lagergrens were waiting for Raoul's plane,
and in the car on the way to their house in Potsdam,
Raoul explained his trip to Budapest:
"to save as many Jews as possible."
And he said in a firm voice:
"It's *urgent* that I leave Berlin
as soon as possible . . . tomorrow!"
Nina, Gunnar, and Raoul talked until midnight.

An hour after they went to bed,

they awoke to the wail of air-raid sirens.

The three watched the Allied planes

come in over the lake by the Lagergrens' house,

headed east to their targets,

then hurried to an underground shelter.

Hours later,

the sirens sounded the all clear.

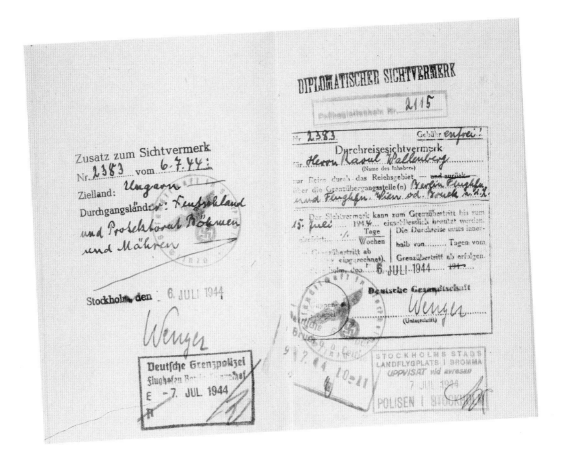

Another page from Raoul's
diplomatic passport.

The next day,

Raoul had lunch at the Swedish legation

with Sweden's minister to Germany, Arvid Richert,

and later went to Berlin's Anhalt Rail Station,

where the platform was crowded with soldiers.
There wasn't an open seat left
on the 5:21 p.m. train to Vienna.
In wartime,
no words ever seem big enough
to hold a family's love.
Raoul hugged his sister goodbye
and squeezed his way into a train car.

From Berlin to Vienna to Budapest,
he sat in the aisle on his rucksacks
and studied a list of names and addresses.
The slow train rumbled across Austria
and then into Hungary.
At the border,
Nazi officials checked Raoul Wallenberg's diplomatic
passport.
Raoul looked at the small swastika in bold ink,
the symbol of such a huge evil,
and hoped that he could make a difference.

ARCHITECT OF
HOPE

JULY 1944

Budapest was a city in the heart of central Europe,
far from the Baltic Sea . . .

and in 1944,

six bridges crossed the Danube River

to connect the two towns that had joined

to form the capital in 1873:

Buda, with its steep hills in the west

and the royal castle where the regent lived,

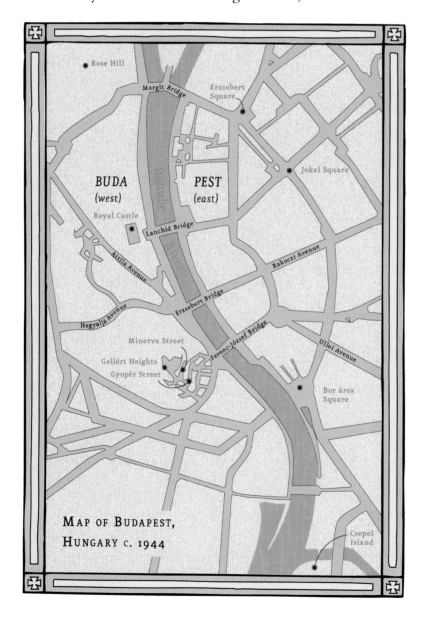

MAP OF BUDAPEST,
HUNGARY c. 1944

The House of
Parliament
in Budapest,
Hungary.

The Fisherman's Bastion in
Budapest.

and Pest, in the east,
with its flat streets
and the tall spires of the Parliament.
On Sunday, July 9,
when Raoul Wallenberg arrived by train,
Budapest was a jewel of a city.
Some called it the "Pearl of the Danube."

When Raoul had visited the capital on his business trips,
one of every ten Hungarians
riding on the orange trams
that clacked along the streets
and crossed the bridges
was Jewish . . .
and just blocks from the Danube,
the Dohány Street Synagogue in Pest,
with its clock towers and cupolas,

was the largest Jewish temple in all of Europe.
Now
life for Jews had changed.

Those in the yellow-star buildings in Pest
had fear in their hearts.
Most of their possessions had been taken by the Nazis.
They had no jobs, and little money.
Other Jews were in hiding,
living with Christian neighbors.

Jews could leave their apartments
only between eleven in the morning and five in the afternoon.
It was difficult to buy food at the markets.
Admiral Horthy had stopped the deportations,
but life was still harsh
for the Jews of Budapest.

On Monday, July 10,
Raoul Wallenberg hurried to the Swedish legation
on Gellért Hill in Buda
with dispatches in his rucksack.
He was to organize rescue efforts for Jews,
but he was given no clear instructions.
His mission was unique . . .
and no one really knew how or if he could succeed.
The yellow mansion
was surrounded by a stone wall with formal gates
and had a rooftop view of the river.
Outside,
on the steep corner of Minerva and Gyopár streets,
there was already a line of stateless Jews

Former Swedish legation
building in Budapest.

risking their curfew
to plead for Swedish protection.

Raoul met with Minister Danielsson
in his elegant office.
During the next few days,
he would meet with Valdemar Langlet of the Swedish Red Cross
and with his old friend Per Anger.
Per had known Raoul in Stockholm
and from his trading trips to Budapest,
and Per's wife, Elena, had known Nina since childhood.
Soon the two young diplomats would work together to save lives.
Raoul's job title, like Per's,
was Secretary of the Swedish legation.

65

Per showed Raoul the letters of protection
that the legation and the Swedish Red Cross
had been giving to Jews.
Raoul studied them carefully.
This was official protection from the Swedish government,
and an essential way to help Jews.
Raoul wanted to grow Per's efforts in a much larger way.
He pulled out his pen and drew a sketch.

Raoul told Per that he had an even *better* idea:
the Swedes would change the letter of protection
into a blue and yellow *passport*.
They would keep the three crowns of Sweden
but add a photo of the passport holder
and the Swedish minister's personal signature.
Raoul hoped that the Nazis
would respect a fancy document.

The two friends decided to call the new document
a *schutzpass* . . .
schutz for protection
and *pass* for passport.
The words on it would be typed
in both German and Hungarian:
This person has plans to travel to Sweden . . .
Until the date of departure,
he and his family and his property
are under the protection
of the Royal Swedish Government.

Each schutzpass was to have a number at the top,
and Minister Danielsson's signature
would give authority to the document.
And . . .
Raoul would record each name and number
in a large black ledger.
He believed that would make the passports legal and official
in the eyes of the Germans.
The Swedes knew they had to bluff the Nazis
and that Raoul needed to print *thousands*
of schutzpasse.
Raoul Wallenberg set up his own department
in two offices on Minerva Street next to the Swedish legation.
Each evening,
he met with Minister Danielsson or Per Anger,
who gave Raoul encouragement and help.

With his list of contacts,
Raoul found good men and women whom he could trust
and offered them jobs and purpose.
Most were Jewish,
and some of them, gathered by Per Anger, had already been working
on behalf of their neighbors.
Hugo Wohl,
Vilmos Forgács,
and others became Raoul's top staff.
His secretaries were Mrs. Falk Lászlóné and Countess Erzsébet Nákó.
None of them spoke Swedish
and Raoul hadn't mastered Hungarian,

so their common language was German.
Within the next few weeks,
there were almost fifty people on Raoul's staff.
Many were volunteers.
Now they
and their families
were under the protection of Sweden.

Raoul Wallenberg's energy spread to others.
He led by example
and never asked anyone to do something
that he refused to do himself.

Some of his staff became typists or printers.
Some were messengers.
Some found typewriters
or candles or flashlights.
Some carried bags of flour and tins of food.
Some purchased medicine and blankets.
Some set up a hospital
and shelters for orphaned children
and schools in the Jewish ghetto.
All reported to the top leaders,
who met daily with Raoul.

Vehicles for civilians were scarce in the city.
Raoul made sure his department's few trucks and cars,
including the black Studebaker that he rented,
were marked with small Swedish flags.
He would use the recognition granted his neutral nation
to travel the streets of Budapest.

The thirty-one-year-old Swedish diplomat was an artist of rescue,
a man of bold ideas, like his grandfather Gustaf.
His one focus was to save as many lives as possible,
and to lessen the huge problems facing the Jews:
hunger,
threats by the Nazis,
disease,
fear and anger,
poverty,
and despair about their own fate.

Jews outside the Swedish legation in Budapest, 1944.

Raoul Wallenberg's personal charm
had always been a magnet
in his family,
with his classmates,
and with those he met in his travels.
Now he used this charisma to lead others,
and as he drew on each of his life skills,

Raoul became the architect
of an extraordinary rescue organization
that was built on courage,
bluff,
thousands of schutzpasse,
and people helping other people who were in trouble.

He didn't have time to save individuals one at a time,
so his goal became saving *groups* of people,
such as extended families.
His idea of *collective passports*
was something that had never been done before.

Top section of a collective schutzpass.

SCHUTZPASSE & SWEDISH HOUSES

AUGUST–OCTOBER 15, 1944

Soon Raoul's pocket calendar and address book
were filled with appointments,
names,
and phone numbers.
Each day he met with other neutral diplomats
and with the Jewish Council,
the Red Cross,
the German SS,
and Hungarian officials . . .
making plans of rescue
or negotiating with the foes of the Jews.

111-681
Gecsö, Lajos, adv. 1800-1900 Zrinyi-u 14
Lederer, Vilma Király-ut 25, 221-207
Israelitisches Waisenkinderhaus
Langlet, Valdemar, 181-578
Levy, Lajos Dr. Jüdisches Spital 223-630
223-684
Laszlo, Lulai Dr. 385-145
Langfeld, Viktor 18-02-25
Galambo-u 7 160-140
Lulai Mester-u 57 III-2
Langlet Üllői-u 32 134-985
Lovasz 6. alt

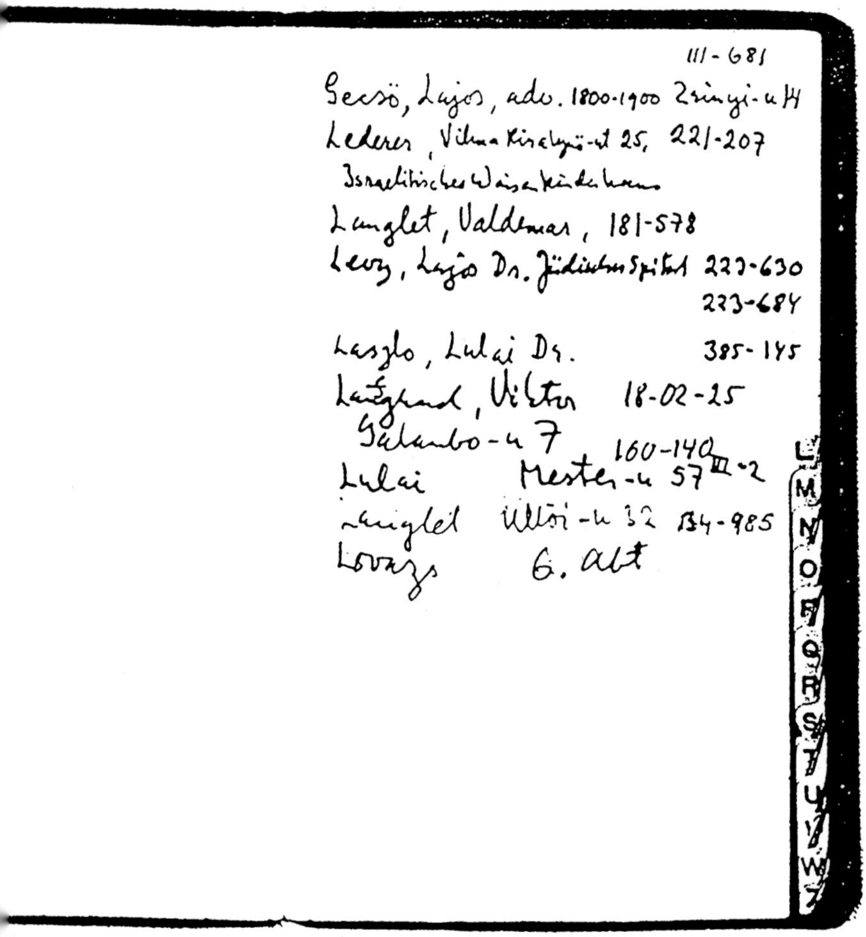

Page from Raoul's address book.

There were many sessions
with the Hungarian government
about *how many people* could have a schutzpass.
The Swedish legation in Budapest
knew that the Nazis would never
allow Jews to travel on trains
through Germany to the sea,
and emigrate via boat to Sweden.
But to stall for time,
and to keep negotiating,
Raoul and Per and Minister Danielsson,
in their meetings with the Hungarian government,
kept using *the idea*
that Jews who held schutzpasse would be departing for Sweden.

Time . . . time . . .

If Raoul's department could just keep the Jews safe
until the Russian army arrived to liberate Budapest . . .
Everyone now knew that Hitler's side
was going to lose the war.

But when?

There were diplomats
in the other neutral legations in Budapest
who were helping the Jews as well:

Carl Lutz from Switzerland,
who was issuing thousands of Swiss papers of protection . . .

Ángel Sanz-Briz from Spain . . .
and his colleague, Giorgio Perlasca, an Italian
businessman who now worked at the Spanish legation . . .

Alberto Carlos de Liz-Teixeira Branquinho of Portugal . . .

Friedrich Born of the International Committee
of the Red Cross . . .

Valdemar Langlet of the Swedish Red Cross
and Asta Nilsson of the International
Committee of the Red Cross . . .

and the Vatican's envoy, Angelo Rotta, who
was more than seventy years old,

and his assistant,
Gennaro Verolino . . .

These good and brave people worked together with Raoul,
and alone.

Soon there were more Swiss,
Spanish,
and Portuguese documents of protection
carried with care in the coat pockets of Budapest's Jews.
But the Swedish schutzpasse with their photos
and the minister's own signature
were the ones most respected by Nazi officials.

Sweden had close trading ties with Hungary,
and the Hungarian government
didn't want to lose them.

A protective pass issued by
the papal nuncio, Angelo
Rotta, in Budapest.

Oltalomlevél

A Római Szentszék Apostoli Követe igazolja, hogy
D e u t s c h Iván / született Budapesten, 1921. november
13-án, Anyja neve : Schäffer Szidónia / a budapesti Apostoli
Nunciatura / pápa követség / védelme alatt áll.

Budapest. 1944 november 13.

NUNZIO APOSTOLICO
/ pápai követ. /

Monsignor Angelo Rotta, a Vatican diplomat
in Sofia and papal nuncio in Budapest.

Gennaro Verolino.

A schutzpass issued by
the Swiss consulate.

SVÁJCI KÖVETSÉG
IDEGEN ÉRDEKEK KÉPVISELETE
KIVÁNDORLÁSI OSZTÁLY
V., VADÁSZ-UTCA 29.

SCHWEIZERISCHE GESANDTSCHAFT
ABTEILUNG FÜR FREMDE INTERESSEN
ABTEILUNG AUSWANDERUNG
V., VADÁSZ-UTCA 29.

480/CL
1944

Die Schweizerische Gesandtschaft, Abteilung fremde Interessen, bescheinigt hiermit,
dass

EGRI TIHAMÉR

im schweizerischen Kollektiv-

A Svájci Követség, Idegen
Érdekek Képviselete, ezennel
igazolja, hogy

EGRI TIHAMÉR

a svájci csoportos (collectiv)
utlevélben szerepel és ezért
nevezett érvényes utlevél bir-
tokában levő személynek tekin-
tendő.

Budapest, 1944. október 23.

A Swedish schutzpass signed
by Carl Ivan Danielsson.

Carlos de Liz-Teixeira Branquinho,
Portuguese chargé d'affaires, in
Budapest in 1944.

The Swiss consul
Carl Lutz, 1944.

Ángel Sanz-Briz, head of the
Spanish legation, in Budapest
in 1944.

There was little business in the capital,

only wartime worry . . .

and air raids,

and rationing of food,

and shortages of electricity,

and, still, the abuses against the Jews.

Some were arrested

or dragged off the streets by anti-Jewish street thugs

and shot.

But there were no deportations to Auschwitz.

Raoul wrote memos of protest with names and details,

and dozens of reports.

Then,
with skilled words and an accusing voice,
Raoul handed these in person to Hungarian officials
in their Buda offices.
"No. 175 . . . No. 176 . . ."

Never before had any diplomat
badgered the Hungarian Foreign Ministry
with so much official paper.
Raoul also wrote dispatches and letters back to Stockholm.
Working on only four or five hours of sleep a night,
he always signed his name
in a bold and urgent scrawl.

On August 6,
two days after his thirty-second birthday,
Raoul sent a note to his mother
via the diplomatic pouch to Sweden:

"We are surrounded by a tragedy
of immeasurable proportions
. . . days and nights are so filled with work
that you are only able to react every now and then . . .
please give my best to Nina and Guy."

SCHUTZ-PASS

Nr. 0390

Name: Éva Balog
Név:

Wohnort: Budapest
Lakás:

Geburtsdatum: 15. Oktober 1910.
Születési ideje:

Geburtsort: Budapest
Születési helye:

Körperlänge: 169 cm.
Magasság:

Haarfarbe: braun   Augenfarbe: grau
Hajszín: Szemszín:

Unterschrift:
Aláírás:

SCHWEDEN

SVÉDORSZÁG

Die Kgl. Schwedische Gesandtschaft in Budapest bestätigt, dass der Obengenannte im Rahmen der — von dem Kgl. Schwedischen Aussenministerium autorisierten — Repatriierung nach Schweden reisen wird. Der Betreffende ist auch in einen Kollektivpass eingetragen.

Bis Abreise steht der Obengenannte und seine Wohnung unter dem Schutz der Kgl. Schwedischen Gesandtschaft in Budapest.

Gültigkeit: erlischt 14 Tage nach Einreise nach Schweden.

A budapesti Svéd Kir. Követség igazolja, hogy fentnevezett – a Svéd Kir. Külügyminisztérium által jóváhagyott – repatriálás keretében Svédországba utazik.

Nevezett a kollektiv útlevélben is szerepel.

Elutazásáig fentnevezett és lakása a budapesti Svéd Kir. Követség oltalma alatt áll.

Érvényét veszti a Svédországba való megérkezéstől számított tizennegyedik napon.

Reiseberechtigung nur gemeinsam mit dem Kollektivpass. Einreisewisum wird nur in dem Kollektivpass eingetragen.

Budapest, den 19. August 1944

KÖNIGLICH SCHWEDISCHE GESANDTSCHAFT
SVÉD KIRÁLYI KÖVETSÉG

Kgl. Schwedischer Gesandte

Antiqua Nyomdai és Irodalmi Rt. Budapest
2367 F. Wiesmeyer Emil

A Swedish schutzpass with Danielsson's signature.

A page from Raoul's pocket calendar.

The days were uncertain,
and the city held its breath
as the summer heat rolled in across the Hungarian plains.
Not far behind, to the east of those plains,
were the tanks of the Russian army.

By September,
Russian troops had crossed the border into Hungary.
Raoul met with his high-ranking
German and Hungarian foes.
Often he flattered these powerful men
and gave them compliments . . .
or threats.
There were rumors that Wallenberg was giving food to Jews,
and helping them obtain Swedish protection.

Some of the Nazis hated Raoul for this
and wanted to arrest him,
or kill him.
Others admired his tenacity and courage
and agreed to some of his demands,
fearing they would be punished for their crimes
when the war was over.

Raoul's humanitarian department
swelled to 115 people.
Officials in the Hungarian government grew restless.
They saw the aid that Raoul had given to the Jews
and the success of his schutzpasse.
They put limits on the number of passports
that the Swedes could issue:
*"Only forty-five hundred Jews are allowed to have these,
and no more!"*

Raoul Wallenberg agreed in his own way.
He wrote names and numbers in his ledger,
from 1 to 4,500,
but since these were collective passports,
often more than one person was protected by each one.
Later he had his staff print up *more* passports.

Each application had to be approved
by a committee of four of Raoul's top staff
before Minister Danielsson signed the schutzpass.
It was crucial to make things look legal
so the Germans would be fooled
by the bold Swedish bluff.

Jews moving from their homes in Budapest.

Raoul began to buy and rent thirty-two apartment buildings.

These were called the "Swedish Houses"

and had signs that read:

THIS HOUSE IS PROTECTED

BY THE ROYAL SWEDISH GOVERNMENT.

On each

hung the Swedish flag.

Wallenberg the architect

knew how to make the most of limited space.

Thousands of Jews with schutzpasse,

and some without,

crowded into buildings that were meant to house hundreds,

and the sight of the blue and yellow flags

near the doorways gave them courage.

The flags of Portugal
and Spain
and Switzerland
and the Red Cross and the Vatican
began to flutter from nearby buildings.

The voices and actions of Raoul Wallenberg
and others
were making a difference.
And . . .
maybe the war would soon be over.

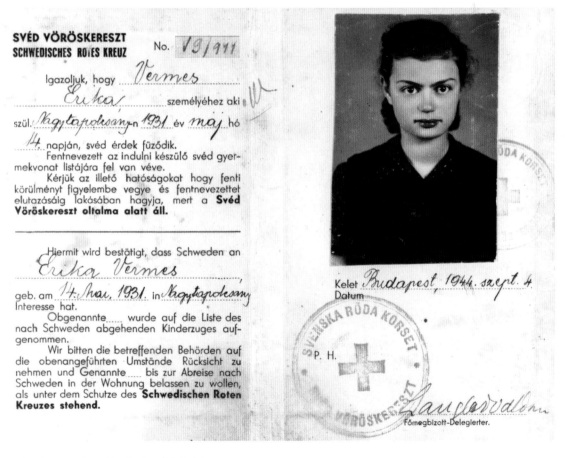

A protective document issued by the Swedish Red Cross.

But in late September,

after getting a frantic phone call,

Raoul rushed west to the Austrian border in his official car.

Hundreds of Jews had been taken there

by the Nazis for forced labor.

Raoul argued with the commandant for four hours,

and finally eighty people,

holding their schutzpasse,

were released.

The calmer days were past.

The fate of the Jews was about to turn again.

THE TERROR OF
THE ARROW CROSS

OCTOBER 15–NOVEMBER 1944

Admiral Horthy had his own plans
to end the war.

On Sunday, October 15,
a day when the distant thunder of Soviet guns
could be heard on the streets of Budapest,
the regent announced a cease-fire.
He was surrendering to the Allies and the Russians.
Hungarians heard this good news on the radio
and church bells began to ring
on both sides of the Danube.

But a few hours later,
everything was turned around.
*"Hungary is **not** surrendering!"*
was the radio announcement,
this time by Arrow Cross leaders.
Spies for the Germans
had known of the regent's plans
and had kidnapped his son.
The SS came to "protect" the old leader.
Admiral Horthy resigned
and was driven away from the palace
under armed guard.

Ferenc Szálasi, the new Hungarian leader,
was a ruthless pro-German
who hated Jews.
Most of his soldiers, the Nyilas, were robbers,
criminals,
and murderers,

and he allowed them to roam the city

in their black Arrow Cross uniforms
and shiny leather boots.
For the next week,
there was no law or order
on the streets of Budapest.
German tanks blocked any traffic.
Jews hid inside their apartments.
The Nyilas had machine guns
and were ready to use them.

The Arrow Cross
after taking power,
October 17, 1944.

Raoul Wallenberg's department
had grown to two hundred people,
and he had moved his offices to Pest.
Dozens of his workers
had been arrested or were in hiding
after the German *putsch,*
or government overthrow,
of October 15.

The new foreign minister of Hungary,
Baron Gábor Kemény,
announced on the radio
that all schutzpasse were no longer valid.

The Arrow Cross stopped Jewish citizens on the street
and tore up their Swedish passes
and threw them in the gutters.
Hundreds of Jews were dragged from the ghetto and shot
or carted away to dig trenches and latrines
for the army.

Quickly,
Raoul made phone calls
and borrowed a lady's bicycle
so that he could get to his buildings.
His steady voice brought calm to rooms filled with panic.
Then Raoul Wallenberg strode into the offices
of the Arrow Cross and the German command,
and demanded the immediate release of his workers.
"These people are under the protection
of the Royal Swedish Government."

That week, on October 17,
a teenager named Thomas Veres
hurried to the Swedish legation on Minerva Street.
His family was Jewish
but had been exempt from the strict laws
because his father had been the personal photographer
of Admiral Horthy.
Now there were *no* exemptions.

Tom Veres in
Budapest.

The young Hungarian had met Per Anger before
and hoped to obtain Swedish protection.

Per knew Tom Veres
because Tom had given lessons to Per's wife,
Elena,
on how to use her camera.
Because Veres also spoke German as well as his native Hungarian,
he soon had a schutzpass and a special letter
stating his new job as Raoul Wallenberg's photographer.
From then on,
Veres would take hundreds of photos for schutzpasse.
Raoul told him:
"You will also document the work we are doing,
and you'll report directly to me."

The invaluable photographs
that Thomas Veres took of Raoul Wallenberg,
his rescue efforts,
and the suffering of the Jews
were sent by diplomatic pouch to Stockholm.
With his camera lens,
Veres was recording tragic history,
and hope.

After October 15,
because the new leaders of the Hungarian government
had stated that the Swedish schutzpasse were null and void,
Raoul Wallenberg and his colleagues at the Swedish legation
knew that something needed to be done,
and *quickly,*
to restore the legality of the protective passes.

Raoul asked the help of a new ally,
the baroness Elisabeth Kemény.
They had met at government receptions
and become friends.
Even though her husband was a devout pro-Nazi,
and a minister in the harsh new government,
the baroness admired Raoul's compassion
and his work to aid Budapest's Jews.
Raoul explained the critical situation
and warned the baroness:
"Your husband may lose his life
when the war is over
and crimes against the Jews are punished."

The beautiful Elisabeth Kemény
firmly asked her husband to reinstate the Swedish schutzpasse.
Gábor Kemény hoped that Sweden
would give diplomatic recognition
to the new leaders of Hungary,
so he gave in to his wife's demands.
A radio announcement was made:
All schutzpasse would again be valid.
The next day,
Raoul Wallenberg sent his friend the baroness
a large bouquet of flowers.

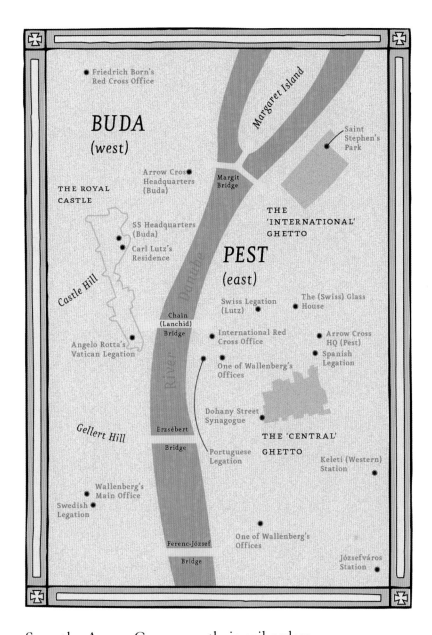

Soon the Arrow Cross gave their evil orders
to the Jews of the city:
Any families who had been exempt
from living in the ghetto
because they held high level jobs
or knew people in the government
were now given six hours

to gather their belongings,
leave their own homes,
and move to the ghetto.
Now!

Almost seventy-two thousand people
lived behind the fences of the Central Ghetto.
The curfew hours had been shortened.
Raoul and others tried to send more food
into the ghetto.
Sanitation was poor.
Air raids were constant.

A few streets north,
the buildings that flew the flags of the neutral countries
became known as the International Ghetto.
Almost thirty thousand more Jews lived here.
Crowded together,
some lived in closets and stairwells.
The brutal members of the Arrow Cross didn't respect any flag.
They robbed and killed
wherever and whenever they wished.

The word *rescue* took on even more urgency.

Raoul's staff swelled to almost four hundred,
including forty doctors.
In Pest,
the families of the staff squeezed into Raoul's office buildings.
Some even slept in the basement vault of the Hazai Bank.
The most fearless on his staff were his trusted fieldworkers.
They risked their lives every day

to go to places where the Arrow Cross gathered Jews,
and then got word to Raoul.

Again and again,
Raoul Wallenberg stood between Jewish families
and their tormentors,
even in the middle of the night.
He hurried to the Arrow Cross prisons,
to the train stations,
to the city brickyard,
to the barges on the Danube,
to wherever the Nazis had dragged groups of terrified Jews.
"These people are under the protection
of the Royal Swedish Government,"
he said again and again.

To the suffering Jews
and to his staff,
he spoke with calm kindness . . .
but when Raoul confronted evil men,
he used loud words of anger
and indignation.
His presence was felt everywhere in Budapest,
and the name Wallenberg always brought hope.

Raoul also drew up a postwar plan
that would help those in the ghettos
find jobs and a return to normal life.
Often he worked at his desk by the light of a flickering candle . . .
and the calendar on the wall behind him
covered a small secret safe.

Raoul Wallenberg
at his desk in
Budapest.

Food began to dwindle in the city
but since July,
Raoul had been buying sacks of flour and other supplies
and hiding them in the cellars of his buildings.
When the battles came closer to Budapest,
he wanted to be prepared.

THE WINTER
DEATH MARCHES

November 1944

There was the terror of the Jews . . .
and there was also the *war*.
By early November,
the Russian army had rolled across the Hungarian plains
and was only a few kilometers
from the suburbs.

Hitler gave strict orders to his army officers in Budapest:
The capital must be held at all costs!
The Germans began to wire the bridges.
If and when the Russian army came into the city,
they would light the fuses and blow them up,
even the Chain Bridge,
just below the royal castle.
It was the most beautiful bridge of all.

The heat of the summer was long past.
The autumn rains and early-winter winds began.
Adolf Eichmann was back in Budapest
to begin the deportations again.
Since there were no more trains to Auschwitz,
Eichmann made another plan to rid Hungary of Jews:
he would force them to *march 240 kilometers on foot*
across the border into Austria and Germany.
If they survived the march,
the Jews would work in labor camps.
Forty thousand people were needed.

Now!

The days of late November 1944

became another black stain on Hungarian history:

Families in Budapest.

Jews of all ages were grabbed from their homes in the ghetto
and marched through the cold streets.
With harsh words and no mercy,
the Arrow Cross and the SS
sent lines and lines of human suffering
onto the dark roads that led west.

By the thousands,
the Jews left Budapest.

One kilometer in fierce winds and rain
or snow
seemed like a thousand kilometers.
Ladies in high heels,
small children,

97

and old men leaning on canes
staggered along the road to Hegyeshalom.
There Eichmann was waiting . . .
to record their names on his lists.
German guards and Arrow Cross henchmen
gave them little food or water, if any,
along the harrowing journey.
Some were allowed to collapse in barns at night along the way,
but most had to sleep in the open fields.
Exhausted,
starved,
and half frozen,
dozens and then more dozens
crumpled by the roadside
and died.

When Raoul's fieldworkers brought news of the marches,
Raoul, Per Anger,
and Lars Berg, another Swedish diplomat,
loaded trucks and their car

Lars Berg by the Swedish
legation in 1944.

with blankets and kettles of hot soup
and slowly drove along the terrible road.
Along the way,
they handed out food and clothing
and tried to rescue those with schutzpasse.
To others,
their voices brought encouragement:
"We shall try to get you back."

The deportation of Jews from the Józsefvárosi train station in Budapest, Hungary, November 1944.

On some trips,
Raoul brought a typewriter
so that one of his staff could type letters of protection
in the back of the truck,
and he set up checkpoints
to trump the Germans
with his own lists and records.

Raoul and other neutral diplomats
also went to the Józsefvárosi train station
and to the Óbuda brickyard,

where the Jews were being collected
before these marches.
Tom Veres was with Wallenberg
and recorded these scenes.
At first he was afraid he would be caught,
but Raoul's courage inspired the young Hungarian.
Tom cut a narrow hole in his woolen scarf
and then hid his Leica camera . . .
pointing the lens through the slit
so that the Nazis wouldn't notice when he took photos.

Many times that November,
unarmed,
Raoul stood on a chair amid the clamor of shouts and beatings
and used a megaphone to call Jews to come forward
with their schutzpasse.
If they had no passports,
Raoul tricked the Germans in a subtle way
and claimed people as Swedish citizens
by using any identity card or scrap of paper
they handed to him.
He told the Nazis:
"I know this man well . . . I personally gave him a passport . . .
Let's not waste our time . . . the line is long . . ."
Seated at a folding table that he often brought with him,
Raoul wrote the Jews' names in his black ledger.
Once Wallenberg climbed on top of a train car
and handed schutzpasse to Jews
through the windows.
The German guards fired warning shots
but were impressed by the Swedish diplomat's courage

so they aimed above his head.

SCHUTZ-PASS

Nr. 28/69.

Name: **Lili Katz**
Név:

Wohnort: **Budapest**
Lakás:

Geburtsdatum: **13.Sept.1913.**
Születési ideje:

Geburtsort: **Budapest**
Születési helye:

Körperlänge: **164 cm.**
Magasság:

Haarfarbe: **blond**   Augenfarbe: **grau**
Hajszín: Szemszín:

Unterschrift:
Aláírás:

SCHWEDEN   SVÉDORSZÁG

Die Kgl. Schwedische Gesandtschaft in Budapest bestätigt, dass der Obengenannte im Rahmen der — von dem Kgl. Schwedischen Aussenministerium autorisierten — Repatriierung nach Schweden reisen wird. Der Betreffende ist auch in einen Kollektivpass eingetragen.

Bis Abreise steht der Obengenannte und seine Wohnung unter dem Schutz der Kgl. Schwedischen Gesandtschaft in Budapest.

Gültigkeit: erlischt 14 Tage nach Einreise nach Schweden.

A budapesti Svéd Kir. Követség igazolja, hogy fentnevezett – a Svéd Kir. Külügyminisztérium által jóváhagyott – repatriálás keretében Svédországba utazik.

Nevezett a kollektiv útlevélben is szerepel.

Elutazásig fentnevezett és lakása a budapesti Svéd Kir. Követség oltalma alatt áll.

Érvényét veszti a Svédországba való megérkezéstől számított tizennegyedik napon.

Reiseberechtigung nur gemeinsam mit dem Kollektivpass. Einreisewisum wird nur in dem Kollektivpass eingetragen.

Budapest, den **25.August**   1944

KÖNIGLICH SCHWEDISCHE GESANDTSCHAFT
SVÉD KIRÁLYI KÖVETSÉG

Kgl. Schwedischer Gesandte

Antiqua Nyomdai és Iroddalmi Rt. Budapest
2267 F. Wiessmayer Emil

A Swedish schutzpass.

The Arrow Cross continued their lawless terror.
Aghast,
Raoul and some of his staff
hurried to the banks of the Danube
during the day and at night
to pull from the icy waters
Jews who had been roped together
and shot.
But for dozens of victims,
the neutral diplomats arrived too late.

In these places of suffering,
Raoul Wallenberg was now the world's eyes and ears.

And he was the world's conscience and voice.

At the Józsefvárosi train station in Budapest in 1944, Raoul (at right, with hands clasped behind his back) rescues Hungarian Jews from deportation by providing them with protective passes.

THE TERRIBLE SIEGE

DECEMBER 1944—JANUARY 17, 1945

In December,
the plight of the Jews grew even worse.
From then on,
Raoul signed hundreds of temporary passes,
papers that stated that the bearer
had applied to receive a schutzpass
and was under protection of the Swedish government.
He used his signature again and again
to save Jewish lives.
R. Wallenberg
R. Wallenberg
R. Wallenberg

Each day became more terrible than the one before it.
The Russians were shelling the city,
or bombing it from the air.
German and Hungarian soldiers were the defenders,
fighting back.
Gangs of black-shirted thugs roamed the streets.
By mid-December,
many in the Arrow Cross government had fled,
including the Baron and Baroness Kemény.
For their safety,
neutral ministers had been recalled to their own countries.
But the other brave diplomats,
including Carl Ivan Danielsson . . .
the only minister to remain . . .
chose to stay in Budapest to help others
and await liberation by the invaders.

Tom Veres was with Raoul Wallenberg
during the long days,

Raoul with his staff in Budapest.

Raoul at his desk.

and he snapped pictures that he developed by candlelight
in his darkroom in the Gerbaud building,
not far from the Hazai Bank.
The teenager risked his life more than once
in carrying multiple copies of these photos
across the square
past Arrow Cross guards.

Finally Raoul told Tom that the danger was too great.
From then on,
the loyal photographer handed Wallenberg rolls
of undeveloped film
and these were sent to Sweden.
Veres even filmed several short movies,
but these were later lost in the chaos of the siege . . .
when it was no longer possible for a courier
to travel to Stockholm.

One of Raoul's Hungarian drivers,
Vilmos Langfelder,
was Wallenberg's constant companion.
The unassuming engineer served as a translator,
and the black Studebaker
that he drove through the streets of Pest
bore the license plate AY152.
But sometimes, to trick Raoul's enemies,
the driver attached different plates
to the back of Wallenberg's car.

On December 20,
there was a small gleam in the ugliness of war:
Raoul was given a Christmas gift by some of his
fieldworkers—
a poem of Hungarian Jewish humor
and an album of hand-painted pictures,
showing the schutzpass throughout the centuries of art.

Vilmos Langfelder, Raoul's driver.

Illustrations from the Christmas
album given to Raoul.

Then,
on Christmas Eve,
the day that Eichmann finally fled from the city,
the terror of the Nyilas struck the Swedish legation in Buda.
The elegant building was looted, its contents broken or stolen,
and the Swedish staff was scattered.
A few days later,
because of firm protests by Raoul Wallenberg,
the legation, with its flag still flying,
was back in Swedish hands
and Hungarian soldiers stood outside the gates
to guard against the street gangs.

After Christmas,
most of the Swedes and the other neutral diplomats
were living in cellars in Buda,
since the bombings made living above ground unsafe.
But Raoul crossed the river to Pest,
sleeping for a few hours each night at a different address:
his offices at the Hazai Bank,
Üllöi Street 2–4,
or apartments whose locations were kept secret.

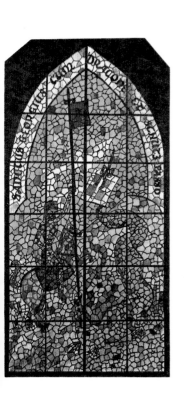

Now the entire city of Budapest was surrounded.
From Berlin,
Hitler sent orders to remind his German soldiers,
and the Hungarian army,
to fight street by street
to hold the city.
When the Russians asked the Germans to surrender,
they refused.

And so the plan for the terrible siege began.

The Russians would bomb the city from the air
and shell it into rubble.
They would destroy the water lines.
They would knock out the electricity.
And . . .
they would starve its defenders to death.
In the 162 buildings of the Central Ghetto
the Jews shivered in their unheated cellars.
Most had only one bowl of soup daily
and a slice of thin bread.
With the poor water supply,
soon the deadly coughing began:
typhus.

Guards outside the
Swedish legation.

In Raoul Wallenberg's thirty-two Swedish houses,
and in the rest of the International Ghetto,
food and medicine were running out.

The Danube was almost frozen,
and the frigid streets were white with drifts of snow
that covered dead Hungarian civilians
and the bones of horses killed for food.
Crazed Nyilas stormed into Swedish houses
and dragged people to the river to be shot.

Raoul Wallenberg and other diplomats
wrote letters of outrage
when infants and children
were carted from their Red Cross shelters
to the Central Ghetto.
But there was no real government left in Budapest
to listen to their pleas . . .
only soldiers fighting other soldiers.

During the two weeks after Christmas,
Raoul met in the town hall
with Pál Szalai, a decent Hungarian
despite his ties to the Arrow Cross.
Pál had contacts with the police
and warned Raoul of dangers to the Jews and the diplomats.
He knew that the Arrow Cross thugs
would kill Raoul if they found him.

In his meetings with Pál Szalai,
Raoul gave the Hungarian permission to use his name
if Szalai heard of any trouble large or small.

On January 10,
Raoul crossed the Danube to see Per Anger in Buda.

Pál Szalai

War-ravaged
Budapest.

Neither of them knew it would be their last meeting together.
Per urged his friend to stay underground
with the other Swedes,
and to give up his rescue work in Pest.
But Raoul told Per:
"I'd never be able to go back to Stockholm
without knowing inside myself
I'd done all a man could do
to save as many Jews as possible."

Together they drove along the shattered streets
to meet with a German Wehrmacht officer,
Gerhard Schmidhuber.
Raoul wanted his promise that those in the ghettos
would not be killed before the liberation.
The general, said Wallenberg,
had the power to do the right thing:

stop a gigantic massacre.

Raoul studied the large wall map
in the hall near the general's office.
German officers constantly charted the progress
of the invading army,
pinning tiny flags on the map to show the Russian advances.

Soon . . .

They would liberate the city soon!

During the cold days of the siege,
Raoul had come to Schmidhuber's command post
several times
in order to look at this map,
and learn which areas of Budapest
the Russians were closing in on.

A few days later,
as the Red Army began to enter Pest,
Pál Szalai heard that Arrow Cross soldiers
and German SS soldiers with machine guns
were about to go ahead with a mass execution.
Unable to contact Raoul Wallenberg,
Szalai told General Schmidhuber
that he would be held responsible
for any terrible acts ordered by others,
and mentioned Wallenberg's name.
This last plan by the Arrow Cross
to murder the Jews of Budapest
was called off by the German commander,
who sent some of his soldiers to arrest the SS
and guard the Central Ghetto.

That week,
on January 13,
Russian soldiers liberated 16 Benczur Street,
a Red Cross transport office in Pest,
and there they met Raoul Wallenberg.
Raoul told them he needed to speak with the top generals
to gain promises that the ghettos would be safe
and given food and medicine
during the liberation of the city.

During the next few days
as the battles raged from street to street,
Raoul gathered his briefcase of postwar plans,
and a suitcase,
and met with some of his staff at an office
and a hospital in Pest,
while Russian soldiers stood outside.

Later,
standing in the lobby of the Hazai Bank
with a small group of loyal friends,
Raoul asked Tom Veres to come with him,
to a meeting with General Malinovsky
in Debrecen, a town 129 miles to the east,
during which Raoul intended to ensure the safety of the ghettos.
But Tom was worried about his missing parents
and wanted to try to search for them.
Raoul understood and wished his friend good luck.

On January 16,
still with his Russian escorts,
Raoul Wallenberg met with László Petö,

Hazai Bank, Harmincad St. #6, in Budapest, 1945. Currently the location of the British Embassy.

the high school summer friend
with whom he'd studied French
and hiked in the Alps
years before.
László lived in Budapest
and during the terrible days
worked as a contact
between Raoul and the Jewish Council.
Raoul gave his friend a warm goodbye
and told him he would return from Debrecen
in a week.

It was snowing in Budapest
when Russian soldiers tore down the wooden fences

113

near the Dohány Street Synagogue
and told the starving Jewish families
that their liberation had finally come.
More than a hundred thousand Jews in the Central and International ghettos
had survived the months of terror.
Germans soldiers and Hungarian street thugs
retreated across the Danube to Buda,
blowing up the stately Chain Bridge on January 18
as they fled amid a crowd of refugees.

Just hours earlier,
on January 17,
Raoul Wallenberg and his driver, Vilmos Langfelder,
set off from Pest not in their usual Studebaker,
but in a blue car,
escorted by three Russian soldiers on a motorcycle,
headed east.
But instead of going to Debrecen,
they were taken to Soviet army intelligence officers
who would not greet them as neutral diplomats
or heroes . . .
but as political enemies
and possible spies for the Americans or the Germans.

Raoul and Vilmos were never seen again
by any of their colleagues,
family,
or friends.

THE MYSTERY OF RAOUL WALLENBERG'S FATE

1945 TO THE PRESENT

From January 17 until February 11, 1945,
fierce street battles were fought on the Buda side of the Danube.
Houses were captured by the Russians
and then won back by the Germans
and then taken by the Russians again.
Almost every building in Buda
was damaged or destroyed.
Over the next months,
drunken Russian victors brought looting, killing, and terror
rather than peaceful liberation
to the civilians of Budapest.

Even in our twenty-first century,
no one knows the entire story of the next chapters
that unfolded in Raoul Wallenberg's life,
although his family and other brave people in the world
have dedicated their lives to seeking the facts
and the truth.

What is known
is that Raoul Wallenberg and Vilmos Langfelder
were taken into custody
and arrested on January 17, 1945,
under the order of the Soviet leader, Joseph Stalin.
They traveled by train with Russian escorts, through Romania
and on to Moscow, where they were given a tour of the subway system.
They then walked to Lubianka Prison,
still under guard,
on February 6, 1945,
and from there to an unknown fate.

On January 16, 1945,
the Soviet government had notified the Swedish minister
in Moscow
that Raoul Wallenberg was in good hands with their army.
Later that spring,
they would deny knowing Raoul Wallenberg,
or where he could be found.
In April of 1945,
when the rest of the Swedish delegation in Budapest
arrived home safely by boat in Stockholm,
Maj von Dardel stood on the quayside,
hoping that Raoul would be with them.
Over the next years,
Maj and Fredrik von Dardel,
helped by friends like Per Anger,
tried to bring their son's missing status
to the attention of Sweden
and the world.

In Lubianka Prison,
Raoul was first held in cell 121,
and then in cell 123.
He told his cellmates that he was in prison
because of a terrible mix-up.
On May 29, 1945,
he was moved to cell 203 in Lefortovo Prison.
According to the scant records that still exist,
he was transferred back to Lubianka in March of 1947.

The Swedish government,

through blunder, fear, and indifference,

never pressed the Russians to admit that Raoul Wallenberg

was somewhere in their prison system.

They turned down an offer of help

from the American government.

In 1947,

a million Swedes signed their names on a petition

to the Russian government,

demanding action on the Wallenberg case.

Due to international pressure,

the Soviets broke their silence on the issue in 1957,

twelve years after Raoul's capture,

and wrote their first public statement,

claiming that Raoul Wallenberg had died of a heart attack

on July 17, 1947, in Lubianka Prison.

Lubianka Prison in Moscow.

Over the next decades,

events in the Soviet Union were shadowed by the Iron Curtain,

but rumors continued to come to the West

from prisoners who had been released from Lubianka,

Vladimir,

and Lefortovo prisons in Russia.

Some stated that he was still alive as a prisoner.

With energy and hope,

Maj and Fredrik von Dardel persisted in efforts

to secure Raoul's freedom

until their deaths a few days apart in 1979

at the ages of eighty-seven and ninety-three.

The Swedish-Russian
Working Group Report.

Two years later, on October 5, 1981,

the United States Congress made Raoul Wallenberg

an honorary U.S. citizen.

Since then,

Nina Lagergren and Guy von Dardel

have met with diplomats and citizens throughout the world

in a quest for the truth from Russian officials.

No proof has ever been found

to verify Raoul Wallenberg's death.

Some think that Raoul was executed in prison long ago.

After the collapse of communism in the Soviet Union,

Nina, Guy, and Per Anger traveled to Moscow in 1989.

Officials there had suddenly "found" a box on a dusty shelf . . .

In it were Raoul Wallenberg's diplomatic passport,

wallet,

address book,

diary,

food coupons,

cigarette case,

Swedish kronor and Hungarian pengoes,

other currencies,

and his driver's license.

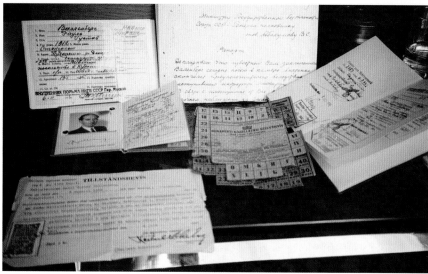

Raoul's personal belongings were returned to his family in 1989.

From 1990 until 2000,

a group of Swedish and Russian diplomats and scholars,

including Guy von Dardel,

studied thousands of documents

and issued a public report

that contains, along with other information,

the testimony of witnesses in the Soviet prison system.
Its findings give few answers
to the many questions about Raoul's fate . . .
and no true timeline for the years after his arrest.

The same Swedish flag that flew above the legation
on Minerva Street,
and whose power of neutrality
Raoul Wallenberg used so well to save tens of thousands of lives,
was riddled by gunfire during the weeks of the siege
and brought back to Stockholm in 1945
by the Swedish Red Cross.
Then the flag was stored away and forgotten by officials
for almost sixty years.

The Swedish flag that flew from the legation in Budapest during the siege (1944–45).

In September of 2004,
Nina Lagergren traveled to Hungary from Sweden
for a ceremony to honor her brother.
With her was the blue and yellow flag,
faded and mended,
carried back to Budapest
as a reminder of a remarkable man's deeds.

The fate of Raoul Wallenberg is still unknown.
His tragic arrest casts a shadow on the light and the hope
that this young Swedish architect brought to those in need
during the dark days of 1944.

His enduring legacy—
the knowledge that one person can make a difference in the world—
lives on in the many thousands whom he and others saved,
and in the generations that follow them.

Others Who Have Made a Difference

CARL LUTZ
Swiss Consul to Hungary
Budapest, Hungary 1944

ARISTIDES de SOUSA MENDES
Portuguese Consul to Bordeaux
Southern France, June 1940

PER ANGER
First Secretary of the Swedish Legation
Budapest, Hungary, 1943–45

MIEP GIES
Office Worker
Amsterdam, Holland, 1940–43

PAUL RUSESABIGINA
Hotel Manager
Rwanda, 1994

HANS DROSSEL
German Judge and Soldier
Germany, 1939–45

JAN KARSKI
Polish Catholic
World War II

SISTER LUISE RADLMEIER
German Catholic Nun
Northern Kenya, 1987–Present

More of Raoul Wallenberg's Life Story

Maj is pronounced as My. Raoul is pronounced as Ra-oul.
Guy is pronounced as G-ee.

Like all Swedes, the Wallenbergs and the von Dardels were
members of the Church of Sweden, a Protestant church
similar to the Lutheran Church in America.

At the University of Michigan, Raoul Wallenberg earned the
Silver Medal in Architecture for the highest grades in his class.

The Hungarian gendarmes who rounded up the Jews
in the countryside from May to June 1944 were not part of
the regular Hungarian army or the city police or the Arrow
Cross Party. They kept order in the countryside and were
feared by many for their cruel ways.

While creating the new schutzpass in July of 1944, Raoul
Wallenberg and Per Anger revised the old Swedish letter
of protection so quickly that they didn't notice a mistake
made by a Hungarian printer: the three crowns of Sweden
were drawn one on top and two below instead of two on top
and one below. The crowns were not corrected, but the
German and Hungarian officials never noticed the error.

The black ledger that Raoul Wallenberg carried during
many rescues was lost or destroyed during the chaotic days
after Budapest's liberation in 1945.

On his birthday on August 4, 1944, Raoul received a leather briefcase and an inkwell as a surprise gift from his staff. He carried this briefcase during rescue efforts in Budapest. Today a bronze briefcase can be seen at the Raoul Wallenberg Memorial in New York City—a symbol of the unfinished work of humanitarians around the world.

The Raoul Wallenberg Memorial in London.

The Raoul Wallenberg Memorial in New York City.

The Raoul Wallenberg Memorial in Stockholm.

During the terrible siege, when Raoul Wallenberg was living in Budapest, he offered his bedroom to a Jewish woman who was about to give birth to a baby. Raoul Wallenberg slept in the hallway in his sleeping bag. After the infant girl was born, Raoul Wallenberg was asked by the new parents to be the baby's godfather. This family survived the war.

In early January of 1945, Raoul Wallenberg met with Giorgio Perlasca, an Italian businessman who was serving bravely as a representative of neutral Spain and helping the Jews of Budapest. Raoul Wallenberg told Giorgio that his life was in danger and asked if he could sleep at the Spanish legation. Perlasca quickly agreed but his friend Raoul never came to the Spanish legation and Giorgio never saw him again.

The Arrow Cross was never recognized as a legal government by any neutral country in Europe. After the war, Pál Szalai, who had assisted with Raoul Wallenberg's efforts, was the only Arrow Cross official not to be charged with war crimes.

Peter Sugar, who wrote the poem for the Christmas album that was given to Raoul Wallenberg as a gift, was killed by the Arrow Cross the day after Raoul received the album. Peter was the only fieldworker to lose his life. After the liberation of Budapest, the Christmas album was found in one of Raoul's rucksacks in the cellar of a Pest office by Lars Berg of the Swedish embassy. When the Swedish group returned to Stockholm, Berg gave the album to Raoul's parents.

After World War II, Per Anger continued to work for the Swedish Foreign Ministry in various countries. Later, he served as the Swedish ambassador to Canada and Australia, and in the years prior to his death in 2002, he supported the efforts of Raoul Wallenberg Committees in cities around the world.

Thomas Veres would learn that his parents had been shot on the banks of the Danube on January 23, 1945. Later he went to America and became a professional photographer in New York City. Tom's office was a few blocks from the United Nations and the Raoul Wallenberg Memorial on First Avenue. In a published interview, Veres said of his work with Raoul: "The fact is that while I was there, I didn't think of the danger. He took you with his kind of thinking. Took you with him." Tom Veres died in 2002.

After saying goodbye to Raoul in Berlin in July 1944, Nina Lagergren soon returned to Stockholm, since she was expecting her first child. Her baby daughter, Nane, was born on October 15, the same day that the Arrow Cross took power in Budapest. After World War II, Gunnar Lagergren had a distinguished judicial career, serving as a highly respected international judge and an arbitrator of disputes between Egypt and Israel, India and Pakistan, and Iran and the United States. He died in 2008 at the age of ninety-six.

In Raoul's last letter to his mother, sent from Budapest during the chaotic days of December, he wrote in the margin, "Lots of kisses to Nina and the little girl."

127

This little girl grew up also to be a citizen of the world. Nane is the wife of Kofi Annan, who served as secretary-general of the United Nations from 1997 to 2006.

Guy von Dardel became a physicist. He spent many years of his life trying to free his half brother from the Soviet prison system, and died in Geneva, Switzerland, in August of 2009 at the age of ninety, after a long illness.

Nina Lagergren at Kappsta, where her brother was born.

Nina and Gunnar Lagergren at their home in Sweden.

The author and Nina Lagergren in Stockholm.

The author and Nane Annan at the United Nations
secretary-general's home in New York.

The author and Guy von Dardel in Geneva, Switzerland.

AUTHOR'S NOTE

The author and Nina walking at Kappsta.

Growing up in America, I had never heard the name Raoul Wallenberg. Years later, I read a book about the life of this Swedish diplomat, and Raoul Wallenberg became my hero. Then by chance during a family visit to Maryland more than a dozen years ago, I met Lee Cochran, an architect in his eighties who had studied at the University of Michigan.

"Did you know Raoul Wallenberg?" I asked.

"Yes, indeed—he was in our class," Lee said. "Everyone called him Rudy."

That afternoon, I promised myself and Lee that I would someday write a book about Raoul Wallenberg.

Since then, I've traveled several times to Sweden to meet with Raoul's sister, Nina. We walked the wooded paths at Kappsta on the island where Raoul was born and drove along the "street of the knight" in Stockholm. I've held Raoul's calendar and address book—brought back from Moscow—in my hands.

I met Raoul's brother, Guy, at his home in Geneva, Switzerland, and made two trips to Budapest to stand by the elegant gates of the former Swedish legation in Buda and cross the Chain Bridge to the apartment buildings in Pest that Raoul rented as his Swedish houses to protect Jews and others under siege.

Andrew Nagy and Gábor Forgács, two long-ago boys who survived the siege, are now my friends, and they have told me their own stories. Andy was twelve years old in 1944 and never met Raoul Wallenberg. He lived at 8 Pannonia Street, which flew a Swedish flag, but his family held Swiss

The author and Andy Nagy in
Ann Arbor, Michigan.

protection papers. Years later he would become a professor at the University of Michigan. Gábor's family lived in a Wallenberg office building and held a schutzpass. His father worked closely with Raoul, and Gábor's younger brother, Paul, helped illustrate the Christmas album that Raoul received as a gift on December 20, 1944.

I don't know the names of the thousands of others who survived because of Raoul Wallenberg's courage, but I do know that these Hungarian Jews have enriched our world with their voices and their art, and with their skills as doctors, teachers, builders, scientists, and leaders. One of those tens of thousands, Tom Lantos, served in the United States Congress for twenty-seven years.

I've seen the Wallenberg memorials in Stockholm and Budapest, in New York City and Ann Arbor, and the bronze statue of Raoul Wallenberg in London, standing with its bearing of courage and hope. Behind him are thousands of schutzpasse in stacks that rise above his head.

I made these journeys as a writer because I wanted to share with others the story of a Swedish schoolboy who grew up to be a hero.

I ask myself, and I ask you: "How can *we* be like Raoul Wallenberg? How can *we* make a difference?"

—*Louise Borden*

The author with Nina and Gunnar at their home in Sweden.

Raoul's 1935 drawing of Riddarholmen for an architectural contest in Stockholm. Note the three crowns on the tower of the city hall.

BIBLIOGRAPHY

What follows is a partial list of sources that assisted me in researching Raoul Wallenberg's life and his months in Budapest.

Adachi, Agnes. *Child of the Winds: My Mission with Raoul Wallenberg.* Chicago: Adams Press, 1989.

Anger, Per. *With Raoul Wallenberg in Budapest: Memories of the War Years in Hungary.* Washington, D.C.: Holocaust Library, United States Holocaust Memorial Museum, 1996.

Berg, Lars. *The Book That Disappeared: What Happened in Budapest.* New York: Vantage Press, 1990. First published in 1949.

Bierman, John. *Righteous Gentile: The Story of Raoul Wallenberg, Missing Hero of the Holocaust.* New York: Penguin Books, 1995.

Cornwell, John. *Hitler's Pope.* New York: Penguin Books, 2008.

Deaglio, Enrico. *The Banality of Goodness: The Story of Giorgio Perlasca.* Notre Dame, Ind.: University of Notre Dame Press, 1998.

Denes, Magda. *Castles Burning: A Child's Life in War.* New York: W. W. Norton & Company, 1997.

Eby, Cecil. *Hungary at War: Civilians and Soldiers in World War II.* State College: Pennsylvania State University Press, 1998.

Ember, Maria. *Wallenberg Budapesten.* Budapest: Varoshaza, 2000.

Finn, David. *Hope: A Monument to Raoul Wallenberg.* Woodstock, N.Y.: Overlook Press, 2000.

Forgacs, Gabor. *Christmas of Raoul Wallenberg.* Budapest: Kolor Optika Kiado, 2004.

———. *Emlek Es Valosag.* Budapest: Katamnak Halaval, 2006.

Fralon, Jose Alain. *A Good Man in Evil Times: The Story of Aristides Sousa Mendes.* New York: Carroll and Graf Publishers, 2001.

Fry, Varian. *Surrender on Demand.* Boulder, Colo.: Johnson Books, 1997. First published by Random House in 1945.

Gann, Christoph. *Raoul Wallenberg: soviel Menschen retten als möglich.* Munich: Verlag C. H. Beck, 1999.

Grove, Andrew S. *Swimming Across.* New York: Warner Books, 2001.

Jalsovszky, Katalin, and Ilona Balog Stemler. *History Written in Light: Photo Chronicle of Hungary 1845–2000.* Budapest: Helikon Publishers, 2001.

Jalsovszky, Katalin, and Emoke Tomsics. *Budapest: The Pearl of the Danube.* Budapest: Helikon Publishers, 2001.

Josephson, Erland, Per Wastberg, Marianne Raberg, et al. *The Soul of Stockholm.* Translated by Joan Tate. Stockholm: Albert Bonniers Forlag, 1999.

Larsson, Jan. *Raoul Wallenberg.* Stockholm: The Swedish Institute, 1995.

Lendvai, Paul. *The Hungarians: A Thousand Years of Victory in Defeat.* Translated by Ann Major. Princeton: Princeton University Press, 2003.

Lester, Elenore. *Wallenberg: The Man in the Iron Web.* Englewood Cliffs: Prentice-Hall, 1982.

Lévai, Jenö. *Raoul Wallenberg: His Remarkable Life, Heroic Battles, and the Secret of His Mysterious Disappearance.* Translated into English by Frank Vajda. West Melbourne: White Ant Occasional Publishing, 1989. First published in Hungarian in 1948.

Levine, Paul A. *Raoul Wallenberg in Budapest: Myth, History and the Holocaust.* London and Portland, Ore.: Vallentine Mitchell, 2010.

Linnea, Sharon. *Raoul Wallenberg: The Man Who Stopped Death.* Philadelphia: Jewish Publication Society, 1993.

Marton, Kati. *Wallenberg: Missing Hero.* New York: Arcade Publishing, 1995.

Nicholson, Michael, and David Winner. *Raoul Wallenberg.* Harrisburg, Pa.: Morehouse Publishing, 1990.

Nylander, Gert, and Anders Perlinge. *Raoul Wallenberg in Documents, 1927–1947.* Stockholm: Banking and Enterprise, 2000.

Raoul Wallenberg: One Man Can Make a Difference Exhibition Catalog. January 25–December 30, 2004. Stockholm: Judiska Museum.

Raoul Wallenberg: Report of the Swedish-Russian Working Group. Stockholm: Ministry for Foreign Affairs, 2000.

Rosenfeld, Harvey. *Raoul Wallenberg: Angel of Rescue.* Buffalo: Prometheus Books, 1982.

Skoglund, Elizabeth R. *A Quiet Courage: Per Anger, Wallenberg's Co-Liberator of Hungarian Jews.* Grand Rapids: Baker Books, 1997.

Survivors of the Shoah Visual History Foundation. *The Last Days.* New York: St. Martin's Press, 1999.

Toland, John. *The Last Hundred Days.* New York: Modern Library , 2003.

Tschuy, Theo. *Dangerous Diplomacy: The Story of Carl Lutz.* Grand Rapids, Mich.: William B. Eerdmans Publishing, 2000.

Ungváry, Krisztián. *The Siege of Budapest: One Hundred Days in World War II.* Translated by Ladislaus Löb. New Haven: Yale University Press, 2002, 2005.

Von Dardel, Maj. *Raoul.* Stockholm: Raben and Sjogren, 1984.

Wallenberg, Raoul. *Letters and Dispatches 1924–1944.* Translated by Kjersti Board. New York: Arcade Publishing, 1995.

The Wallenberg Book Committee. Edited by Penny Schreiber and Joan Lowenstein. *Remembering Raoul Wallenberg.* Ann Arbor: University of Michigan Press, 2001.

Werbell, Frederick E., and Thurston Clarke. *Lost Hero: The Mystery of Raoul Wallenberg.* New York: McGraw-Hill, 1982.

ARCHIVE SOURCES

Bentley Library, Ann Arbor, Michigan

Harlan Hatcher Graduate Library, University of Michigan, Ann Arbor, Michigan

United States Holocaust Memorial Museum, Washington, D.C.

Raoul Wallenberg Foundation, Stockholm, Sweden

National Archives and Records Administration Washington, D.C. and College Park, MD.

Library of Congress

From the United States Holocaust Memorial Museum Archives:

Oral history interview with Per Anger
October 21, 1986
Call number: RG-50.462*0001

Oral history interview with Per Anger
March 12, 1990
Call number: RG-50.244*0008

Oral history interview with Per Anger
January 19, 1995
Call number: RG-50.030*0301

Oral history interview with Thomas Veres
August 28, 1989
Call number: RG-50.244*0153

Oral history interview with Pál Szalai
March 26, 1990
Call number: RG-50.244*0163

Oral history interview with Giorgio Perlasca
November 3–5, 1989
Call number: RG-50.244*0126

Oral history interview with
Baroness Elisabeth Kemény Fuchs
May 15, 1986
Call number: RG-50.462*0008

VIDEO RECORDINGS

Raoul Wallenberg: Buried Alive
Rubicon Films Production, 1984
Includes oral statements by Elisabeth Kemény,
Lars Berg, and Per Anger.

Nina Lagergren's Wallenberg Lecture
University of Michigan, October 25, 2000

Per Anger's Wallenberg Lecture
University of Michigan, 1995

Raoul Wallenberg 50th Anniversary
Remembrance
Washington, D.C., 1995
Includes remarks by Per Anger,
Guy von Dardel, and Thomas Veres.

ACKNOWLEDGMENTS

The author would like to thank the following people for their gracious meetings, phone conversations, letters, translations, and steady encouragement:

In Europe:

Nina and Gunnar Lagergren – Stockholm

Mi Lagergren Ankarcrona – Stockholm

Louise von Dardel – Paris

Guy and Matti von Dardel – Geneva

Gabor and Kati Forgacs – Budapest

Elena Anger – Stockholm

Harald Hamrin – Swedish Foreign Ministry/Stockholm

Jan Lundvik – Stockholm and Budapest/former Swedish Ambassador to Hungary

Erik Blegvad – London

In the United States:

Irene Butter – Ann Arbor/RW Medal Committee

Andrew Nagy – Ann Arbor/RW Medal Committee

Lee and Elizabeth Cochran – Sykesville, Maryland

Nane Annan – New York City

Adele Veres – Scarsdale, New York

Swedish Embassy – Washington, D.C.

Caroline Waddell, Nancy Hartman and Michlean Amir – The United States Holocaust Memorial Museum

Also, with much gratitude:

my husband Pete and our children, Cate, Ayars, and Ted

Florence Heide, Maryann Macdonald, Trish Marx, Johanna Hurwitz, Pat Giff, M. K. Kroeger, G. E. Lyon, and Stephanie Harvey

Margaret K. McElderry

patient travel agent Mary Ann Iemmola

Alex and Cindy Curchin, who went to Kappsta with me, and who crossed the border at Hegyeshalom

the design team at HMH, Rachel Newborn, and Yay!Design

and to my wonderful editors Amy Flynn, Kate O'Sullivan, and, especially, Erica Zappy.

PHOTO CREDITS